Unearthing Genocides Impact on Humanity

Copyright Page

TITLE: Unearthing the Truth: Genocides and Their Impact on Humanity

1ST Edition

Table of Contents

Unearthing the Truth: Genocides and Their Impact on Humanity

By Roberto Miguel Rodriguez

Chapter 1: Historical Genocides: A Focus on Specific Instances of Genocide throughout History

The Holocaust: A Systematic Genocide against Jews in Nazi Germany

Introduction:

The Holocaust stands as one of the most horrific and systematic acts of genocide in human history. This subchapter will delve into the details of the Holocaust, focusing on the persecution and extermination of Jews in Nazi Germany. By exploring the historical context, methods employed and the impact on humanity, this chapter aims to provide historians with a comprehensive understanding of this dark chapter in our collective past.

Historical Context:

The Holocaust occurred during World War II when Adolf Hitler's Nazi regime rose to power in Germany. Hitler's anti-Semitic ideology fueled a systematic campaign against Jews, resulting in their dehumanization, persecution, and eventual extermination. This chapter will explore the historical factors that contributed to the rise of the Nazis and the implementation of their genocidal policies.

Methods and Implementation:

The Nazi regime employed a range of methods to carry out the systematic genocide of Jews. From the establishment of concentration camps to the implementation of the Final Solution, this subchapter will analyze the methods used to identify, segregate, and ultimately exterminate millions of Jews. It will also examine the complicity of various institutions and individuals in facilitating the genocide.

Impact on Humanity:

The Holocaust had far-reaching consequences that continue to reverberate throughout society. This subchapter will explore the profound impact of the Holocaust on individuals, communities, and the collective memory of humanity. It will also consider the long-term effects on survivors, their descendants, and the global Jewish community.

Relevance to Historians:

Understanding the Holocaust is crucial for historians specializing in historical genocides. By examining the specifics of this particular instance, historians can gain valuable insights into the mechanisms and patterns of genocidal acts. Furthermore, this chapter will provide valuable historical context for the study of genocide prevention and intervention, genocide survivors and their stories, and the legal frameworks surrounding genocidal crimes.

Conclusion:

The Holocaust remains a stark reminder of the depths of human cruelty and the importance of studying and understanding historical genocides. By delving into the systematic genocide against Jews in Nazi Germany, this subchapter aims to enrich the knowledge and understanding of historians and shed light on the lasting impact of this tragic chapter in human history.

The Armenian Genocide: The Massacre of Armenians by the Ottoman Empire

Introduction:

The Armenian Genocide stands as one of the most tragic and horrific instances of mass atrocities in human history. Occurring during the final years of the Ottoman Empire, it resulted in the systematic extermination of an estimated 1.5 million Armenian civilians. This subchapter delves into the details and consequences of this genocide, shedding light on the events that unfolded between 1915 and 1923.

Historical Context:

To understand the Armenian Genocide, it is essential to examine the geopolitical and cultural factors that led to its occurrence. The Ottoman Empire, facing internal strife and external pressure, embarked on a policy of ethno-religious homogeneity, with Armenians becoming a target due to their Christian faith and perceived disloyalty. The empire's decline, coupled with rising nationalism and the First World War, created fertile ground for the genocide.

The Genocide:

The Armenian Genocide was characterized by widespread deportations, forced labor, starvation, and outright massacres. Under the guise of relocation, Armenians were forcibly removed from their homes and sent on death marches to desert regions where they faced extreme hardships. Along the way, they were subjected to brutal violence, rape, and torture. These acts were perpetrated by Ottoman authorities, military units, and local militias.

International Response:

The international community's response to the Armenian Genocide was largely inadequate. Despite mounting evidence of the atrocities, political interests and fears of destabilizing the Ottoman Empire hindered any substantial intervention. While some nations condemned the genocide, no meaningful action was taken to prevent or halt the atrocities. The lack of intervention set a dangerous precedent for future genocides.

Denial and Revisionism:

In the aftermath of the Armenian Genocide, the Ottoman Empire and its successors engaged in a systematic campaign of denial and revisionism. This phenomenon, which continues to this day, seeks to distort or erase the historical occurrence of the genocide. Genocide denial not only insults the memory of the victims but also perpetuates a cycle of violence and prevents true reconciliation.

Conclusion:

The Armenian Genocide serves as a stark reminder of the horrors that human beings are capable of inflicting upon one another. Its impact on the Armenian people and their collective memory is profound and continues to shape their identity. By studying and acknowledging this genocide, historians play a crucial role in the pursuit of justice, prevention of future genocides, and the preservation of human rights.

The Rwandan Genocide: Ethnic Cleansing and Mass Killing of Tutsis by Hutus

The Rwandan Genocide is a dark chapter in human history that cannot be forgotten. It was a brutal and systematic campaign of ethnic cleansing and mass killing, targeting the Tutsi minority by the majority Hutu population. This subchapter aims to provide a comprehensive understanding of the Rwandan Genocide, examining its causes, consequences, and the international response.

The origins of the Rwandan Genocide can be traced back to the colonial era when Belgium ruled over Rwanda. The Belgian authorities exacerbated existing tensions between the Hutus and Tutsis by favoring the latter, creating a divide that would ultimately lead to violence. The genocide itself occurred between April and July 1994, resulting in the deaths of approximately 800,000 people, mostly Tutsis but also moderate Hutus who opposed the violence.

The subchapter will delve into the events leading up to the genocide including the assassination of President Juvenal Habyarimana, which served as a catalyst for the violence. It will explore the systematic nature of the killings, with Hutu militias and civilians actively participating in the extermination of Tutsis. The role of the media in fueling hatred and inciting violence will also be examined, highlighting the dangerous power of propaganda.

Furthermore, the subchapter will discuss the international community's response, or lack thereof, to the genocide. Despite early warnings and pleas for intervention, the United Nations and other world powers failed to take decisive action, allowing the massacres to continue unabated. This raises important questions about the responsibility to protect and the role of global powers in preventing genocides.

The subchapter will also shed light on the aftermath of the genocide and the challenges faced by Rwandan society in its efforts towards reconciliation and healing. It will explore the establishment of the International Criminal Tribunal for Rwanda, which sought to hold perpetrators accountable for their crimes, as well as the role of truth and reconciliation commissions in promoting justice and healing.

Lastly, the subchapter will touch upon the significance of the Rwandan Genocide in the broader context of genocidal atrocities throughout history. It will emphasize the importance of remembering and learning from such tragedies to prevent future instances of genocide. By analyzing the Rwandan Genocide through the lens of historical genocides, this subchapter aims to contribute to the understanding of genocide as a global phenomenon and its impact on humanity.

Other Modern Genocides

The Bosnian Genocide

The Bosnian Genocide, which occurred during the Bosnian War from 1992 to 1995, was a tragic and brutal conflict characterized by mass killings, ethnic cleansing, and widespread atrocities. It took place in the context of the breakup of Yugoslavia and the struggle for control over Bosnia and Herzegovina, a multi-ethnic country with a significant Bosniak (Bosnian Muslim), Bosnian Serb, and Bosnian Croat population.

Here are some key points about the Bosnian Genocide:

1. Background: The breakup of Yugoslavia in the early 1990s resulted in several ethno-nationalist conflicts across the region. In Bosnia and Herzegovina, tensions among the various ethnic groups escalated into a full-scale war after the country declared independence from Yugoslavia in 1992.

2. Ethnic Cleansing: The Bosnian Genocide involved systematic campaigns of ethnic cleansing, primarily carried out by Bosnian Serb forces under the leadership of figures like Radovan Karadžić and Ratko Mladić. They aimed to create ethnically homogeneous territories by forcibly removing and killing Bosniak and Bosnian Croat civilians. Massacres, forced deportations, and concentration camps were used as methods to achieve this goal.

3. Srebrenica Massacre: One of the most notorious events of the Bosnian Genocide was the Srebrenica Massacre in July 1995. Bosnian Serb forces captured the town of Srebrenica, which had been declared a United Nations Safe Area, and subsequently killed approximately 8,000 Bosniak men and boys in a matter of days. It is considered the largest mass murder in Europe since World War II.

4. Siege of Sarajevo: Sarajevo, the capital of Bosnia and Herzegovina, was besieged by Bosnian Serb forces for nearly four years, from 1992 to 1996. During this time, the city

endured heavy shelling and sniper attacks, resulting in a large number of civilian casualties.

5. International Response: The Bosnian Genocide prompted international outrage and led to the intervention of NATO forces in 1995. The Dayton Agreement, signed in December 1995, ended the Bosnian War and established the framework for peace in Bosnia and Herzegovina. The International Criminal Tribunal for the Former Yugoslavia (ICTY) was also established to prosecute those responsible for war crimes, crimes against humanity, and genocide.

6. War Crimes Trials: Many individuals, including political leaders, military commanders, and other figures, were indicted and tried for their roles in the Bosnian Genocide by the ICTY in The Hague. Notable cases include Radovan Karadžić, Ratko Mladić, and Slobodan Milošević.

The Bosnian Genocide remains a deeply painful and complex chapter in European history, and its legacy continues to impact the region. Efforts at reconciliation, justice, and rebuilding have been ongoing since the end of the war, but challenges persist in addressing the deep scars left by the conflict.

The Cambodian Genocide

The Cambodian Genocide, which occurred from 1975 to 1979 under the rule of the Khmer Rouge regime led by Pol Pot, is one of the most devastating and horrific genocides of the 20th century. During this period, the Khmer Rouge attempted to transform Cambodia into an agrarian, communist society, resulting in the deaths of an estimated 1.7 million people through execution, forced labor, and famine. Here are some key details about the Cambodian Genocide:

1. Rise of the Khmer Rouge: The Khmer Rouge, a communist

guerrilla group, seized power on April 17, 1975, following years of civil war in Cambodia. Under the leadership of Pol Pot, they aimed to create an agrarian, classless society by eliminating perceived enemies of the state and eradicating urban and intellectual elements.

2. Evacuation of Cities: Shortly after taking power, the Khmer Rouge forcibly evacuated the urban population of Cambodia, including Phnom Penh, into the countryside. This massive displacement was part of their plan to create a purely agrarian society. Families were separated, and people were subjected to brutal treatment during the evacuation.

3. Forced Labor: Once in the countryside, the urban population was forced into labor camps, where they were subjected to grueling and inhumane labor. People were put to work in rice fields, building infrastructure, and engaging in other physically demanding tasks, often with insufficient food and medical care. Those who couldn't work were often executed.

4. Mass Executions: The Khmer Rouge conducted mass executions of perceived enemies of the state, including intellectuals, professionals, political opponents, and ethnic and religious minorities. Killing fields, where mass executions took place, were scattered throughout Cambodia. The victims were often bludgeoned to death, shot, or killed in other brutal ways.

5. Torture and Brutality: Torture and brutality were widespread in the Khmer Rouge's prisons and detention centers, such as Tuol Sleng (S-21). Prisoners were subjected to torture and forced to confess to crimes they did not commit. Very few who entered these facilities survived.

6. Famine and Disease: The forced collectivization of agriculture, along with poor planning and mismanagement, led to food shortages and famine. People were often denied adequate nutrition, and as a result, many succumbed to starvation and

disease.

7. Vietnamese Intervention: In December 1978, Vietnam invaded Cambodia and overthrew the Khmer Rouge regime. The Vietnamese intervention put an end to the worst of the atrocities, although sporadic fighting continued for several years.

8. Legacy: The Cambodian Genocide left deep scars on Cambodia. The country lost a significant portion of its population, and survivors faced physical and psychological trauma. The Khmer Rouge's rule also left Cambodia with a shattered infrastructure and a traumatized society.

9. International Tribunals: In the 2000s, international efforts, including the United Nations-backed Extraordinary Chambers in the Courts of Cambodia (ECCC), were established to prosecute senior Khmer Rouge leaders for their roles in the genocide. Some key figures, including Pol Pot's chief executioner Kaing Guek Eav (Duch), were brought to trial and sentenced.

The Cambodian Genocide remains a painful and haunting chapter in world history, and its effects continue to be felt in Cambodia today as the country seeks justice, reconciliation, and healing.

The Darfur Genocide

The Darfur Genocide refers to a conflict that began in the early 2000s in the Darfur region of western Sudan, where the Sudanese government and government-backed militias carried out a brutal campaign of violence against non-Arab ethnic groups, primarily the Fur, Zaghawa, and Massalit communities. This campaign resulted in widespread atrocities, including mass killings, rape, forced displacement, and other crimes against humanity. Here are some key details about the Darfur Genocide:

1. Background: The conflict in Darfur has complex historical, ethnic, and political roots. It emerged as a response to long-standing grievances related to land, resources, and representation. The region had suffered from droughts and desertification, exacerbating competition for arable land and water resources.

2. Ethnic and Political Dimensions: The Darfur conflict is often characterized as an ethnic and political conflict. Non-Arab ethnic groups, which felt marginalized and discriminated against by the central Sudanese government dominated by Arab elites, formed rebel groups to seek greater autonomy and representation.

3. Janjaweed Militias: In response to the rebellion, the Sudanese government armed and supported Arab militias known as the Janjaweed. These militias were responsible for many of the brutal attacks against Darfur's non-Arab communities. They targeted villages, burned homes, raped women, and killed civilians indiscriminately.

4. Mass Displacement: The conflict resulted in one of the largest internal displacements of people in the world. Hundreds of thousands of Darfuris were forced to flee their homes and seek refuge in internally displaced persons (IDP) camps or across the border in neighboring Chad. These IDP camps faced dire humanitarian conditions.

5. International Response: The international community, including the United Nations, condemned the violence in Darfur and deployed peacekeeping forces, such as the African Union-United Nations Hybrid Operation in Darfur (UNAMID), to protect civilians and provide humanitarian assistance.

6. Genocide Allegations: The term "genocide" has been used by various organizations and individuals to describe the violence

in Darfur. In 2004, the United States government officially labeled it as genocide. The United Nations has described the situation as "crimes against humanity" and "war crimes." The determination of whether the violence constitutes genocide has been a subject of debate and controversy.

7. Ongoing Conflict: While the intensity of the conflict in Darfur has decreased since its peak in the mid-2000s, sporadic violence and insecurity persist. Peace agreements have been signed and efforts to achieve reconciliation continue, but many challenges remain.

8. Accountability: The International Criminal Court (ICC) issued arrest warrants for several individuals, including Sudanese President Omar al-Bashir, for their alleged roles in the Darfur conflict. Some individuals have been arrested and brought to trial, but others remain at large.

The Darfur Genocide remains a complex and ongoing issue, with a need for continued international attention and efforts to address the root causes, provide justice to victims, and promote lasting peace and reconciliation in the region.

The Guatemalan Genocide

The Guatemalan Genocide, which took place during the Guatemalan Civil War from the early 1960s to the mid-1990s, was a protracted and brutal conflict marked by mass killings, forced disappearances, and widespread human rights abuses. The conflict primarily occurred between the Guatemalan military and government-backed paramilitary groups against leftist guerrilla groups and perceived sympathizers, particularly indigenous Mayan communities. Here are key details about the Guatemalan Genocide:

1. Historical Background: The Guatemalan Civil War had deep-

rooted causes, including political instability, socioeconomic
inequality, land disputes, and ethnic tensions. Indigenous
Mayan communities in Guatemala had long suffered
discrimination and land dispossession.

2. Military Coup (1954): In 1954, a U.S.-backed military coup
   ousted the democratically elected government of Jacobo
   Árbenz, marking the beginning of a series of authoritarian
   regimes in Guatemala. This coup set the stage for decades of
   political violence and repression.

3. Counterinsurgency and Repression: In the early 1960s, leftist
   guerrilla movements emerged in response to oppressive
   government policies. The Guatemalan military, under various
   dictatorships, launched counterinsurgency campaigns that
   targeted not only guerrilla fighters but also civilian populations
   perceived as supporting them.

4. Massacres and Forced Disappearances: The Guatemalan
   military and paramilitary groups carried out massacres in
   indigenous villages suspected of harboring guerrillas or
   sympathizing with them. These massacres often involved the
   deliberate killing of civilians, including women and children.
   Forced disappearances, in which people were abducted and
   never seen again, were also widespread.

5. Scorched Earth Campaigns: The Guatemalan military
   implemented scorched earth campaigns in which entire villages
   were destroyed, crops were burned, and livestock were killed.
   These campaigns aimed to deprive guerrillas of support and
   punish suspected sympathizers.

6. U.S. Involvement: The United States played a significant role in
   supporting the Guatemalan military during the civil war. U.S.
   military aid, training, and political support were provided to
   successive Guatemalan governments, despite evidence of
   widespread human rights abuses.

7. Truth Commission and Peace Accords: As the civil war continued, international pressure mounted on Guatemala to address human rights abuses. In 1996, peace negotiations led to the signing of the peace accords, formally ending the conflict. A Truth Commission was established to investigate past atrocities and recommend measures for reconciliation.

8. Accountability and Justice: Efforts to hold perpetrators accountable for the genocide and other human rights abuses have been ongoing. In 2013, former Guatemalan dictator Efraín Ríos Montt was convicted of genocide and crimes against humanity, although his conviction was later overturned on a technicality.

9. Ongoing Challenges: Despite the end of the civil war, Guatemala continues to face challenges related to reconciliation, justice, and addressing the legacy of the genocide. Indigenous communities, in particular, continue to seek justice and reparations for the violence they endured.

The Guatemalan Genocide remains a deeply painful and contentious chapter in the country's history. Efforts to achieve justice and reconciliation are ongoing, with a focus on addressing the root causes of the conflict and promoting the rights and well-being of marginalized communities, especially the indigenous Mayan population.

The Kurdish Genocide in Iraq

The Kurdish Genocide in Iraq refers to a series of systematic and brutal campaigns conducted by the regime of Saddam Hussein, the President of Iraq, against the Kurdish population in northern Iraq during the late 1980s. These campaigns resulted in mass killings, forced deportations, and the use of chemical weapons against Kurdish civilians, primarily those belonging to the Kurdish ethnic group. Here are key details about the Kurdish Genocide in Iraq:

1. Background: The conflict between the Iraqi government and
   the Kurdish population in northern Iraq had deep historical
   roots. Kurds, who are an ethnic minority, had long sought
   greater autonomy and recognition of their cultural and
   political rights within Iraq.
2. Anfal Campaigns: The Kurdish Genocide is often associated
   with the "Anfal" campaigns, which were a series of eight
   military operations conducted by the Iraqi government
   between 1986 and 1989. These campaigns were named after a
   Quranic verse and were intended to crush Kurdish resistance
   and eliminate perceived support for Kurdish rebel groups,
   particularly the Patriotic Union of Kurdistan (PUK) and the
   Kurdistan Democratic Party (KDP).
3. Chemical Attacks: One of the most infamous aspects of the
   Kurdish Genocide was the use of chemical weapons by Iraqi
   forces. The most well-known chemical attack occurred in
   March 1988 in the town of Halabja, where thousands of
   Kurdish civilians were killed, and many more suffered severe
   health consequences. Chemical weapons, such as mustard gas
   and nerve agents, were also used in other areas.
4. Mass Killings and Mass Graves: The Iraqi military and security
   forces conducted mass killings of Kurdish civilians during the
   Anfal campaigns. Villages were targeted, and residents were
   often executed en masse. Many victims were buried in mass
   graves, which have been discovered in various locations in
   northern Iraq.
5. Forced Displacement: The regime forcibly displaced Kurdish
   communities from their ancestral lands, leading to the
   destruction of villages and towns. Families were separated, and
   many were placed in resettlement camps under harsh
   conditions.
6. International Response: The atrocities committed during the

Kurdish Genocide drew international condemnation. The United Nations and various human rights organizations documented the crimes and called for accountability. The international community provided humanitarian assistance to Kurdish refugees.

7. Aftermath and Justice: Following the fall of Saddam Hussein's regime in 2003, efforts were made to document and investigate the atrocities committed during the Kurdish Genocide. Trials of key figures, including Saddam Hussein himself, were conducted. Saddam Hussein was found guilty of crimes against humanity and was executed in 2006.

8. Legacy: The Kurdish Genocide left a profound impact on the Kurdish population and the region as a whole. It remains a deeply painful and significant chapter in the history of Iraqi Kurdistan, and the memory of the genocide continues to shape Kurdish identity and political aspirations.

The Kurdish Genocide in Iraq serves as a stark reminder of the devastating consequences of state-sponsored violence and the importance of international efforts to hold perpetrators accountable for such atrocities.

The Rohingya Genocide

The Rohingya Genocide refers to the systematic campaign of violence and persecution against the Rohingya Muslim minority in Myanmar (Burma) carried out by the Myanmar military and security forces. This campaign has resulted in mass killings, widespread displacement, sexual violence, and other atrocities, leading to a humanitarian crisis of immense proportions. Here are key details about the Rohingya Genocide:

1. Background: The Rohingya are a predominantly Muslim

ethnic group in Myanmar, primarily residing in the Rakhine State in the western part of the country. For decades, they have faced discrimination, marginalization, and statelessness, with the Myanmar government denying them citizenship and basic rights.

2. Escalation of Violence: The recent wave of violence against the Rohingya can be traced back to 2012 when communal violence erupted between Rohingya Muslims and ethnic Rakhine Buddhists in Rakhine State. This violence escalated over time, leading to a series of military crackdowns and campaigns against the Rohingya.

3. 2017 Crackdown: The most significant and brutal crackdown occurred in August 2017 when the Myanmar military, responding to attacks by Rohingya insurgents on security forces, launched a large-scale offensive against Rohingya communities. This military campaign resulted in mass killings, widespread rape, and the burning of Rohingya villages.

4. Mass Killings: Thousands of Rohingya civilians, including men, women, and children, were killed during the 2017 crackdown. Mass graves have been discovered in Rakhine State, providing evidence of the scale of the atrocities.

5. Forced Displacement: The violence in 2017 triggered one of the largest forced migrations in recent history. Hundreds of thousands of Rohingya fled to neighboring Bangladesh, creating a massive refugee crisis. Today, there are over a million Rohingya refugees living in overcrowded and squalid refugee camps in Bangladesh.

6. Sexual Violence: Reports and testimonies from survivors indicate that sexual violence, including rape, was systematically used as a weapon of war during the crackdown. Women and girls were particularly vulnerable to such abuses.

7. Denial of Citizenship and Rights: The Myanmar government

has long denied the Rohingya citizenship and the associated rights, effectively rendering them stateless. Discriminatory policies, restrictions on movement, and limited access to education and healthcare have been used to further marginalize the Rohingya.

8. International Response: The Rohingya Genocide has prompted widespread international condemnation. The United Nations and human rights organizations have described it as ethnic cleansing and genocide. The International Court of Justice (ICJ) issued provisional measures in 2020, calling on Myanmar to take steps to prevent further harm to the Rohingya.

9. Ongoing Crisis: The crisis continues to unfold, with Rohingya refugees facing dire living conditions in refugee camps in Bangladesh and limited prospects for safe return to Myanmar. Efforts to secure justice and accountability for those responsible for the genocide are ongoing.

The Rohingya Genocide represents a grave violation of human rights and international law, and it has had a profound impact on the Rohingya population and the region. It underscores the urgent need for international action to address the root causes of the crisis, provide justice for the victims, and work toward a sustainable and peaceful solution for the Rohingya people.

The South Sudanese Genocide

The South Sudanese Civil War, which began in December 2013, is a complex and devastating conflict that has resulted in widespread violence, displacement, and human suffering. While the conflict has been marked by serious human rights abuses and atrocities, it is important to note that the classification of the South Sudanese conflict as a "genocide" is a subject of debate and has not been officially determined by international bodies. Nonetheless, the war has had significant humanitarian and human rights implications. Here are key details about the South Sudanese Civil War:

1. Background: South Sudan became an independent nation in July 2011, following decades of civil war with Sudan. However, tensions within South Sudan's political leadership, primarily between President Salva Kiir and former Vice President Riek Machar, escalated into open conflict in December 2013.

2. Ethnic Dimensions: The South Sudanese Civil War has had strong ethnic dimensions, with President Kiir belonging to the Dinka ethnic group and Riek Machar to the Nuer ethnic group. The conflict quickly took on ethnic undertones, leading to violence between communities.

3. Humanitarian Crisis: The conflict has had devastating humanitarian consequences. It has resulted in the displacement of millions of people, both internally and as refugees in neighboring countries. Food insecurity, malnutrition, and a lack of access to healthcare have been widespread.

4. Atrocities and Human Rights Abuses: Numerous reports and investigations have documented serious human rights abuses during the conflict, including mass killings, sexual violence, recruitment of child soldiers, and the destruction of civilian infrastructure.

5. Peace Agreements: The South Sudanese Civil War has seen several attempts at peace negotiations. The most significant was the signing of the Agreement on the Resolution of the Conflict in South Sudan (ARCSS) in 2015, which led to a transitional government. However, these agreements have often been fragile, and violence has continued.

6. International Response: The international community has expressed deep concern about the conflict and has supported

peace efforts through diplomacy, sanctions, and humanitarian assistance. The United Nations Mission in South Sudan (UNMISS) has played a role in protecting civilians and facilitating humanitarian aid.

7. Challenges to Accountability: Achieving accountability for the atrocities committed during the conflict has been challenging. Efforts to establish a hybrid court to prosecute individuals responsible for human rights abuses have faced obstacles.

8. Ongoing Conflict: The South Sudanese Civil War has gone through phases of violence, ceasefires, and renewed fighting. While there have been some positive developments in terms of peace agreements, the situation remains fragile, with sporadic violence and tensions between various armed groups.

The South Sudanese Civil War is a deeply tragic and ongoing crisis with profound humanitarian implications. While the conflict's categorization as a genocide is debated, it is clear that it has resulted in immense human suffering and has had a significant impact on the stability and development of South Sudan as a nation. Efforts to address the conflict, provide humanitarian aid, and seek accountability for human rights abuses continue to be vital.

Chapter 2: Genocide Denial and Revisionism: Exploring the Phenomenon of Denying or Revising Historical Occurrences of Genocides

Denial of the Holocaust: Conspiracy Theories and Anti-Semitic Narratives

In the study of historical genocides, one cannot ignore the disturbing phenomenon of Holocaust denial. Despite overwhelming evidence and testimonies, there are individuals and groups who propagate conspiracy theories and anti-Semitic narratives, seeking to revise or deny the historical occurrence of the Holocaust. This subchapter delves into the origins, motivations, and impact of Holocaust denial, shedding light on its dangers and exploring responses to combat this disturbing trend.

Holocaust denial is rooted in deep-seated anti-Semitism and has gained traction through the dissemination of misinformation and revisionist narratives. This subchapter examines the various conspiracy theories surrounding the Holocaust, such as claims that it was a Jewish fabrication to gain sympathy or that the number of Jewish victims was greatly exaggerated. By analyzing these theories, historians can debunk them with evidence, demonstrating the fallacies and dangers they pose.

The phenomenon of Holocaust denial not only distorts historical truth but also perpetuates anti-Semitism and hate crimes. This subchapter highlights the impact of Holocaust denial on Jewish communities and the broader implications for human rights and social cohesion. By exploring the relationship between denial and the resurgence of anti-Semitism, historians can contribute to the understanding of contemporary challenges and the importance of countering hate speech and discrimination.

Efforts to combat Holocaust denial and revisionism are essential for ensuring the preservation of historical truth and preventing the recurrence of genocidal acts. This subchapter examines strategies and initiatives aimed at countering denial, including education, legislation, and the use of technology to disseminate accurate information. By studying successful interventions, historians can contribute to the development of effective tools and methods to combat denial in other instances of genocide.

Ultimately, this subchapter seeks to emphasize the importance of acknowledging and addressing Holocaust denial within the broader context of historical genocides. By understanding the motivations, tactics, and impact of denial, historians can actively contribute to the ongoing fight against hate speech, discrimination, and the revision of historical atrocities. Through their research and advocacy, historians can ensure that the victims and survivors of genocides are never forgotten, and their stories continue to be heard as a testament to the resilience of humanity in the face of unimaginable horrors.

Denial of the Armenian Genocide: Turkish Government's Official Position

The denial of the Armenian Genocide by the Turkish government is a contentious and highly debated topic within the realm of historical genocides. Despite overwhelming evidence and consensus among scholars, the Turkish government has maintained an official position of denial, refusing to acknowledge the systematic extermination of 1.5 million Armenians during World War I.

The Turkish government's denial of the Armenian Genocide can be traced back to the immediate aftermath of the atrocities. In the years following the genocide, the Ottoman Empire, which was responsible for the mass killings, went through a period of political turmoil and eventually transformed into modern-day Turkey. With this transformation, a concerted effort was made to suppress any discussion or recognition of the genocide.

The Turkish government's official position argues that the events of 1915-1923 were not a deliberate campaign of extermination targeting the Armenian population, but rather a result of the chaotic conditions of World War I. They claim that the deaths were a result of inter-ethnic conflict, famine, and disease, rather than a premeditated genocide.

Despite the overwhelming evidence to the contrary, the Turkish government has employed various tactics to maintain this official position. These tactics include the intimidation of scholars and journalists who dare to speak out about the genocide, as well as the promotion of revisionist narratives that seek to downplay or deny the scale and intent of the atrocities.

The denial of the Armenian Genocide by the Turkish government is not only an act of historical revisionism but also a violation of human rights. By denying the genocide, the Turkish government perpetuates a culture of impunity, denying justice to the victims and their descendants. It also hinders the process of reconciliation and healing in post-genocide societies, as acknowledgment and truth-telling are crucial steps towards building a more inclusive and peaceful future.

In conclusion, the Turkish government's official position on the denial of the Armenian Genocide is a highly controversial and deeply flawed stance. Despite overwhelming evidence and international consensus, the Turkish government continues to suppress the truth and deny justice to the victims. It is imperative for historians and the international community to continue shining a light on this denial, seeking truth, and advocating for the recognition of the Armenian Genocide.

Denial of the Rwandan Genocide: The Role of Ethnic Politics and Propaganda

In the wake of the Rwandan Genocide, a disturbing phenomenon emerged: denial of the atrocities that had taken place. This subchapter delves into the role of ethnic politics and propaganda in perpetuating this denial, shedding light on the complex dynamics that hindered acknowledgment and reconciliation.

Ethnic politics played a crucial role in laying the groundwork for genocide denial. The pre-existing ethnic divisions in Rwandan society were exploited by those in power, who used propaganda to fuel animosity and create an environment conducive to violence. By promoting a narrative that dehumanized the Tutsi minority, the Hutu-dominated government further polarized the population and justified the mass murder that followed.

Propaganda campaigns were key in shaping public opinion and manipulating historical memory. Radio stations such as RTLM became instruments of hate, broadcasting dehumanizing messages and inciting violence against Tutsis. These media outlets, controlled by the government and extremist Hutu groups, disseminated false narratives that portrayed the genocide as a defensive act against a Tutsi-led rebellion. By distorting the historical record and manipulating emotions, these propaganda campaigns sought to erase the truth and perpetuate denial.

The subchapter also explores the international response to genocide denial. Despite overwhelming evidence and testimonies from survivors, some individuals and groups persisted in denying the atrocities or revising the historical occurrence of the genocide. This denial not only caused further pain to the survivors but also hindered efforts towards justice and reconciliation.

The subchapter concludes by emphasizing the importance of countering genocide denial through education, research, and legal mechanisms. Historians play a crucial role in unearthing the truth and challenging revisionist narratives. By engaging with survivor testimonies, archival evidence, and scholarly research, historians can provide a counter-narrative to denial and contribute to the collective memory of genocide.

Addressing genocide denial requires a multifaceted approach that includes promoting human rights, supporting survivors, and fostering reconciliation. By understanding the role of ethnic politics and propaganda in denial, historians can contribute to the broader discussion on genocide prevention, intervention, and justice.

This subchapter will be of particular interest to historians specializing in the Rwandan Genocide and those exploring the phenomenon of genocide denial and revisionism. It offers valuable insights into the complex dynamics at play and the challenges faced in acknowledging and reckoning with historical genocides.

Chapter 3: Genocide Prevention and Intervention: Examining Strategies and Initiatives Aimed at Preventing and Intervening in Instances of Genocide

Early Warning Systems: Identifying Genocide Risk Factors and Early Signs

In the study of historical genocides, it is essential to understand the factors that contribute to the occurrence of such atrocities. By identifying the risk factors and early signs of genocide, historians can better comprehend the mechanisms that lead to mass violence and work towards preventing future atrocities. This subchapter aims to delve into the intricate web of genocide risk factors and early warning signs, shedding light on the crucial role they play in understanding and addressing genocidal acts throughout history.

Genocide is not a spontaneous event; it is often preceded by a series of warning signs and risk factors. By analyzing historical genocides such as the Holocaust, Armenian Genocide, and Rwandan Genocide, historians can identify common patterns and indicators that foreshadowed these horrific events. These risk factors can include socio-political tensions, discrimination, dehumanization, and the erosion of human rights. By recognizing these factors, historians can provide valuable insights into the conditions that create a breeding ground for genocide.

Equally important are the early signs that precede genocidal acts. These signs can manifest in various forms, such as hate speech, propaganda, targeted violence, and the marginalization of specific groups. By closely examining these early indications, historians can alert societies and policymakers to the potential for genocide, allowing for timely intervention and prevention.

Understanding the risk factors and early signs of genocide is not only important for historians but also for individuals and organizations working in genocide prevention and intervention. By studying historical instances of genocide, experts can develop effective strategies and initiatives aimed at identifying and addressing these risk factors before they escalate into mass violence.

Moreover, the insights gained from analyzing historical genocides can influence legal frameworks and mechanisms related to prosecuting genocidal crimes and seeking justice for victims. By understanding the root causes and warning signs, legal professionals can strengthen international laws and tribunals to hold perpetrators accountable for their actions.

In conclusion, the study of early warning systems is a crucial aspect of understanding and preventing genocide. By identifying the risk factors and early signs, historians can contribute to the fields of genocide prevention and intervention, international law, human rights, reconciliation, and media representation. With this knowledge, societies can work collectively to ensure that the dark chapters of history are not repeated, and the rights and dignity of all individuals are protected.

International Criminal Court: Prosecution of Genocide Perpetrators

The International Criminal Court (ICC) plays a crucial role in the global fight against impunity for genocide perpetrators. Established in 2002, the ICC is the first permanent international tribunal with jurisdiction over the most serious crimes of concern to the international community, including genocide, crimes against humanity, war crimes, and the crime of aggression. This subchapter will delve into the important work of the ICC in prosecuting individuals responsible for committing genocide.

The ICC's mandate is to investigate and prosecute those who bear the greatest responsibility for the commission of these crimes, regardless of their official capacity or the country in which the crimes were committed. This is a significant development in international law, as it ensures that individuals cannot escape justice by hiding behind state sovereignty.

Through its investigations and prosecutions, the ICC seeks to bring justice to the victims of genocide and prevent future atrocities. By holding perpetrators accountable, the ICC aims to deter potential genocidal actors and contribute to the prevention of such crimes.

One of the significant challenges faced by the ICC is the apprehension and arrest of suspects. Cooperation from member states is crucial in this regard, as the ICC relies on their support to execute arrest warrants and transfer individuals to its custody. This subchapter will explore the complexities and limitations of international cooperation in bringing genocide perpetrators to justice.

Furthermore, the subchapter will examine some of the landmark cases prosecuted by the ICC, such as those related to the Rwandan Genocide, Darfur conflict, and the ongoing situation in Myanmar. These cases serve as important examples of the ICC's role in seeking justice for victims and highlighting the gravity of genocide as a crime against humanity.

Lastly, the subchapter will discuss the impact of the ICC's work on the overall fight against genocide. It will analyze the effectiveness of the court in deterring future genocidal acts, promoting accountability, and providing redress to victims. Additionally, it will consider the challenges and criticisms faced by the ICC, including issues of resource allocation, political interference, and limitations in its jurisdiction.

Overall, this subchapter aims to provide historians with a comprehensive understanding of the ICC's role in prosecuting genocide perpetrators. It will shed light on the legal frameworks and mechanisms employed by the ICC, the challenges it faces in its mission, and the impact of its work on the prevention and intervention in instances of genocide.

United Nations and Peacekeeping Missions: Protecting Vulnerable Populations

In the face of atrocities and violence inflicted upon vulnerable populations, the United Nations has played a crucial role in peacekeeping missions around the world. From preventing genocides to intervening in ongoing conflicts, the UN's efforts have aimed to protect those who are most at risk. This subchapter will delve into the United Nations' involvement in peacekeeping missions and its impact on vulnerable populations throughout history.

Throughout the 20th and 21st centuries, the United Nations has been actively engaged in preventing and responding to genocides and other mass atrocities. With a mandate to maintain international peace and security, the UN has deployed peacekeeping forces to conflict zones, providing protection and assistance to vulnerable populations.

One notable example of the UN's peacekeeping efforts is the Rwandan Genocide in 1994. As thousands of innocent lives were being mercilessly taken, the UN Security Council authorized the deployment of peacekeeping forces to Rwanda. However, due to limited resources and a lack of political will, their intervention fell short, resulting in devastating consequences. This case serves as a reminder of the challenges faced by the UN in protecting vulnerable populations during genocidal crises.

Despite setbacks, the UN has made significant strides in improving its peacekeeping operations. Today, peacekeeping missions include a strong mandate to protect civilians, with a particular focus on vulnerable populations such as women, children, and refugees. The UN has also recognized the importance of engaging local communities and promoting peacebuilding initiatives to prevent the recurrence of violence.

In addition to peacekeeping missions, the UN has played a pivotal role in prosecuting genocidal crimes and seeking justice for victims. International courts and tribunals, such as the International Criminal Tribunal for Rwanda and the International Criminal Court, have been established to hold perpetrators accountable. These legal frameworks, supported by the UN, aim to ensure that the victims' voices are heard and that justice is served.

By examining the United Nations' involvement in peacekeeping missions, this subchapter sheds light on the organization's commitment to protecting vulnerable populations. It explores the challenges faced by the UN in preventing genocides, the progress made in peacekeeping operations, and the importance of pursuing justice for victims. Through an analysis of historical cases and lessons learned, historians can gain a deeper understanding of the UN's role in safeguarding human rights and preventing mass atrocities.

Chapter 4: Genocide Survivors and Their Stories: Highlighting the Experiences and Testimonies of Survivors from Different Genocides

Holocaust Survivors: Bearing Witness to the Horrors of Nazi Genocide

The Holocaust stands as one of the most horrific and widely recognized genocides in history. The systematic murder of six million Jews, along with millions of other victims, by the Nazis during World War II left an indelible mark on humanity. In this subchapter, we delve into the experiences and testimonies of Holocaust survivors, who have played a pivotal role in unearthing the truth and ensuring that the horrors of the Nazi genocide are never forgotten.

Holocaust survivors provide a unique perspective on the atrocities committed during this dark period of history. Their firsthand accounts bear witness to the unimaginable suffering, loss, and dehumanization that took place in concentration camps, ghettos, and death marches. Through their stories, historians gain valuable insights into the complex dynamics of Nazi genocide and the resilience of the human spirit in the face of unimaginable evil.

These survivors have played a crucial role in countering denial and revisionism surrounding the Holocaust. By sharing their stories, they challenge those who seek to distort or deny the historical reality of this genocide. Their testimonies provide irrefutable evidence of the systematic extermination of millions of innocent lives, serving as a powerful reminder of the consequences of hatred, bigotry, and indifference. Holocaust survivors have become advocates for truth and justice, ensuring that the memory of the Holocaust remains alive and that future generations learn from this dark chapter in human history.

Furthermore, the testimonies of Holocaust survivors have had a profound impact on efforts towards reconciliation and healing in post-genocide societies. Through their stories, they humanize the victim and create empathy among individuals and nations. Their narratives have paved the way for truth and reconciliation commissions, which aim to confront the past, acknowledge the crimes committed, and foster dialogue and understanding between victims and perpetrators.

The stories of Holocaust survivors have also shaped the representation of genocides in various forms of media. Films, documentaries, and literature have provided a platform for survivors to share their experiences with a global audience, ensuring that their stories are not confined to the pages of history books. These narratives have played a crucial role in educating the public and preserving the memory of the Holocaust, making it impossible to forget the horrors that occurred.

In conclusion, Holocaust survivors have played a vital role in unearthing the truth about the Nazi genocide. Their testimonies have challenged denial and revisionism, contributed to reconciliation and healing, and shaped the representation of genocides in various forms of media. As historians, it is our duty to listen to their stories, document their experiences, and ensure that their voices continue to be heard, so that the lessons of the Holocaust are never forgotten.

Armenian Genocide Survivors: Preserving Cultural Identity in the Face of Genocidal Atrocities

The Armenian Genocide stands as one of the most devastating instances of mass violence and systematic extermination in history. From 1915 to 1923, the Ottoman Empire targeted the Armenian population, resulting in the deaths of an estimated 1.5 million Armenians. Despite the immense loss and trauma endured, many Armenian genocide survivors have demonstrated remarkable resilience in preserving their cultural identity and heritage.

This subchapter explores the experiences of Armenian genocide survivors and their ongoing efforts to maintain their cultural identity in the face of genocidal atrocities. By examining their stories, we gain invaluable insights into the human capacity for resilience and the enduring power of cultural heritage.

The Armenian Genocide survivors faced immense challenges in the aftermath of the atrocities. Many were forcibly displaced, with their communities destroyed and their homes confiscated. Yet, despite these hardships, they refused to let go of their cultural identity. They sought refuge in various countries, establishing diaspora communities that became centers for preserving Armenian culture.

Language, religion, and traditional practices played a crucial role in maintaining their cultural identity. Armenian genocide survivors made conscious efforts to pass down their language, Armenian Christianity, and cultural traditions to future generations. Through the transmission of oral histories, music, dance, and cuisine, they ensured the survival of Armenian culture and its integration into their new environments.

The Armenian diaspora also played a significant role in raising awareness about the Armenian Genocide and combating denial and revisionism. Through grassroots activism, community organizations, and lobbying efforts, survivors and their descendants fought for recognition and justice. Their tireless advocacy led to the establishment of genocide memorials, museums, and educational programs worldwide, ensuring that the Armenian Genocide would never be forgotten.

In conclusion, the resilience and determination of Armenian genocide survivors in preserving their cultural identity in the face of unimaginable horrors serve as a testament to the indomitable spirit of humanity. Their stories transcend time and inspire us to confront the dark chapters of history, challenge denial and revisionism, and work towards preventing future genocides. By understanding their experiences, historians can contribute to the broader discourse on historical genocides and their impact on humanity.

Rwandan Genocide Survivors: Rebuilding Lives amidst Trauma and Loss

The Rwandan Genocide, one of the most devastating instances of genocide in history, left an indelible mark on the survivors who managed to escape the brutality. Their stories of resilience and determination to rebuild their lives amidst trauma and loss are both heartbreaking and inspiring. This subchapter delves into the experiences of Rwandan genocide survivors, shedding light on their struggle for justice, healing and reconciliation.

The Rwandan Genocide took place between April and July 1994, when approximately 800,000 Tutsis and moderate Hutus were systematically murdered by extremist Hutus. The survivors, known as "Ibuka" or "those who remember," faced unimaginable horrors, witnessing the slaughter of their loved ones and enduring physical and psychological trauma themselves. Many were forced to flee their homes and seek refuge in crowded camps or foreign countries.

Despite the immense challenges they faced, Rwandan genocide survivors have shown remarkable resilience in rebuilding their lives. Through testimonies and personal accounts, this subchapter explores their journeys of healing and recovery. It highlights the efforts of survivors to seek justice for the crimes committed against them and their loved ones, including their participation in legal proceedings and their advocacy for the recognition of the genocide.

Moreover, the subchapter delves into the role of survivors in the reconciliation process in post-genocide Rwanda. It examines the establishment of truth and reconciliation commissions, which aimed to bring together survivors and perpetrators in an effort to promote understanding, forgiveness, and healing. The subchapter also explores the challenges faced by survivors in the aftermath of the genocide, such as the stigmatization and discrimination they continue to endure.

By shedding light on the experiences and stories of Rwandan genocide survivors, this subchapter aims to contribute to the broader discussion on the impact of genocides on individuals and societies. It underscores the importance of recognizing and acknowledging the resilience of survivors in the face of unimaginable atrocities. Additionally, it emphasizes the need for continued support and resources to aid in the healing and rebuilding process for survivors of genocidal violence.

Through this exploration, historians and readers interested in the field of historical genocides will gain a deeper understanding of the specific challenges faced by Rwandan genocide survivors and the ongoing efforts towards justice, healing, and reconciliation in post-genocide Rwanda. The subchapter serves as a testament to the strength and resilience of the human spirit, even in the face of unimaginable tragedy.

Chapter 5: Genocide and International Law: Analyzing Legal Frameworks and Mechanisms Related to Prosecuting Genocidal Crimes and Seeking Justice for Victims

The Genocide Convention: Definition and Legal Obligations

Introduction:

The Genocide Convention, officially known as the Convention on the Prevention and Punishment of the Crime of Genocide, is a crucial international legal instrument that defines and prohibits acts of genocide. Adopted by the United Nations General Assembly in 1948, this convention has played a vital role in shaping the global response to genocidal crimes. This subchapter explores the definition of genocide as outlined in the convention and delves into the legal obligations it imposes on states.

Defining Genocide:

The Genocide Convention defines genocide as any of the following acts committed with the intention to destroy, in whole or in part, a national, ethnic, racial, or religious group: killing members of the group, causing serious bodily or mental harm to members of the group, deliberately inflicting conditions of life to bring about its physical destruction, imposing measures to prevent births within the group, and forcibly transferring children of the group to another group.

Legal Obligations:

The convention places several legal obligations on states party to it. These obligations include preventing and punishing acts of genocide, enacting laws that make genocide a crime under their domestic legislation, and cooperating with international efforts to prevent and punish genocide. States are also required to extradite or prosecute individuals accused of committing acts of genocide, regardless of their nationality or where the crime was committed.

Challenges and Implications:

While the Genocide Convention represents a significant step towards preventing and punishing genocide, its implementation has faced challenges. Genocide denial and revisionism have hindered efforts to acknowledge historical instances of genocide. Additionally, the convention's reliance on state cooperation and the lack of an international enforcement mechanism have limited its effectiveness in holding perpetrators accountable.

Conclusion:

The Genocide Convention serves as a critical tool in addressing genocidal crimes and seeking justice for victims. By providing a clear definition of genocide and imposing legal obligations on states, the convention contributes to the prevention and punishment of these heinous acts. However, ongoing challenges, such as denial and revisionism, highlight the importance of continued research, education, and advocacy within the field of historical genocides. Historians play a crucial role in unearthing the truth and promoting understanding, ensuring that the lessons from past genocides inform efforts towards prevention, intervention, reconciliation, and justice in the future.

International Criminal Tribunals: Adjudicating Genocide Cases

The establishment of international criminal tribunals has played a crucial role in addressing and prosecuting genocidal crimes throughout history. These tribunals serve as a mechanism to seek justice for victims and hold perpetrators accountable for their actions. In this subchapter, we will explore the significance of international criminal tribunals in adjudicating genocide cases, shedding light on the legal frameworks and mechanisms related to prosecuting genocidal crimes and seeking justice for victims.

One of the most notable international criminal tribunals is the International Criminal Tribunal for the former Yugoslavia (ICTY) which was established by the United Nations in 1993. The ICTY has been instrumental in prosecuting individuals responsible for the genocide in Srebrenica, the ethnic cleansing in Bosnia and Herzegovina, and other genocidal acts committed during the Yugoslav Wars. Through its work, the ICTY has not only brought justice to victims but has also helped establish an important precedent for future tribunals.

Another significant international criminal tribunal is the International Criminal Tribunal for Rwanda (ICTR), established in 1994 in response to the Rwandan Genocide. The ICTR has been instrumental in prosecuting those responsible for the mass killings and sexual violence that occurred during the genocide. By holding trials and delivering verdicts, the ICTR has played a vital role in promoting accountability and ensuring that the perpetrators of these heinous crimes are brought to justice.

These international criminal tribunals have faced numerous challenges in their pursuit of justice. They have encountered difficulties in gathering evidence, locating and apprehending suspects, and ensuring fair trials. However, their efforts have paved the way for the establishment of the International Criminal Court (ICC), which serves as a permanent institution for prosecuting individuals accused of genocide, war crimes, and crimes against humanity.

The establishment of international criminal tribunals has not only contributed to the legal prosecution of genocidal crimes but has also served as a deterrent to future atrocities. These tribunals send a powerful message that those who commit genocide will be held accountable for their actions. Moreover, they provide a platform for survivors to share their stories, ensuring that their voices are heard and their experiences acknowledged.

In conclusion, international criminal tribunals have played a crucial role in adjudicating genocide cases. They have helped bring justice to victims, hold perpetrators accountable, and establish legal precedents for future prosecutions. By examining the legal frameworks and mechanisms related to prosecuting genocidal crimes, we can gain a deeper understanding of the importance of these tribunals in seeking justice and preventing future atrocities.

Truth and Justice: Balancing Prosecution and Reconciliation in Post-Genocide Societies

In the aftermath of genocidal atrocities, societies are often left grappling with the complex task of seeking truth and justice while simultaneously working towards reconciliation. This subchapter delves into the delicate balance between prosecution and reconciliation in post-genocide societies, exploring the challenges and potential solutions that arise in the pursuit of both.

Historians specializing in historical genocides, such as the Holocaust, Armenian Genocide, or Rwandan Genocide, play a crucial role in shedding light on the truths of these horrific events. Their research and analysis provide a foundation for understanding the scale, causes, and consequences of genocides, as well as the imperative for justice.

However, the pursuit of justice is not without its challenges. Genocide denial and revisionism pose significant obstacles, as individuals or groups attempt to distort or erase the historical occurrence of genocides. Historians must confront these deniers and revisionists, countering their claims with irrefutable evidence and ensuring that the truth remains accessible and widely acknowledged.

Genocide survivors and their stories also play a pivotal role in this subchapter. By highlighting the experiences and testimonies of survivors from different genocides, historians can humanize the atrocities and provide a voice to those who have suffered immeasurable loss. These personal narratives serve as a powerful reminder of the need for justice and reconciliation.

The subchapter explores the legal frameworks and mechanisms related to prosecuting genocidal crimes and seeking justice for victims. It delves into the complexities of international law and how it can be utilized to hold perpetrators accountable. Additionally, it examines the impact of genocide on human rights, including issues of ethnic and religious discrimination, further emphasizing the importance of justice in post-genocide societies.

Efforts towards reconciliation and healing in post-genocide societies are also examined, including truth and reconciliation commissions. These commissions provide a platform for victims and perpetrators to come together, allowing for the acknowledgement of past wrongs, the pursuit of justice, and ultimately, the possibility of reconciliation. The subchapter analyzes the successes and challenges of these initiatives and explores the role they play in the broader context of post-genocide societies.

This subchapter concludes by examining the representation of genocides in media. It analyzes how films, documentaries, and literature shape public understanding and memory of genocides, and the potential impact this has on the pursuit of justice and reconciliation.

In summary, the subchapter "Truth and Justice: Balancing Prosecution and Reconciliation in Post-Genocide Societies" explores the intricacies and challenges of seeking both justice and reconciliation in the aftermath of genocidal atrocities. It highlights the crucial role of historians, survivors, and legal frameworks in this process, and delves into the impact of media representation on our collective memory of genocides. By addressing these complex issues, this subchapter contributes to a deeper understanding of the legacies of historical genocides and their impact on humanity.

Chapter 6: Genocide and Human Rights: Discussing the Impact of Genocide on Human Rights, Including Issues of Ethnic and Religious Discrimination

Ethnic Cleansing: Violations of the Right to Ethnic Identity and Cultural Heritage

The subchapter titled "Ethnic Cleansing: Violations of the Right to Ethnic Identity and Cultural Heritage" delves into the devastating impact of ethnic cleansing on the fundamental rights of individuals and communities. This chapter aims to provide historians with a comprehensive understanding of the historical genocides that targeted specific ethnic groups, such as the Holocaust, Armenian Genocide, or Rwandan Genocide, and the severe consequences they had on the victims' cultural heritage and ethnic identity.

Throughout history, genocides have systematically targeted certain ethnic groups with the intention of eradicating their cultural and historical existence. This subchapter explores the methods employed in these instances, including forced assimilation, destruction of cultural artifacts, prohibition of language and religious practices, and displacement of populations. By doing so, it highlights the deliberate attempts to erase the victims' ethnic identity and cultural heritage, ultimately stripping them of their sense of belonging and robbing future generations of their history.

The chapter delves into the psychological and emotional toll that ethnic cleansing inflicts on survivors, as they grapple with the loss of their cultural heritage and struggle to preserve their identity in the face of adversity. It also examines the role of collective memory in the aftermath of genocides, exploring how societies remember and commemorate these atrocities, often through the establishment of memorials, museums, and educational programs.

Furthermore, this subchapter explores the intersectionality of gender in the context of ethnic cleansing, shedding light on the unique experiences of different genders during genocides. It discusses the targeting of women and the use of sexual violence as a weapon of genocide, emphasizing the need for a gender-sensitive approach in understanding and addressing these crimes.

Drawing from international law and human rights frameworks, this chapter analyzes the legal mechanisms and initiatives aimed at prosecuting genocidal crimes and seeking justice for the victims. It also examines the efforts towards reconciliation and healing in post-genocide societies, including truth and reconciliation commissions, which play a crucial role in addressing the deep wounds inflicted by ethnic cleansing.

By delving into these crucial aspects of ethnic cleansing and their impact on the right to ethnic identity and cultural heritage, this subchapter provides historians with a comprehensive analysis of historical genocides and their lasting implications for humanity.

Religious Persecution: Targeting Religious Minorities during Genocides

Religious persecution has been a recurring theme throughout history, particularly during instances of genocide, where religious minorities have often been targeted and subjected to unimaginable atrocities. Understanding the role of religious persecution within genocides is crucial for historians and those interested in delving deeper into the complexities of historical genocides.

Throughout history, genocides have shown a consistent pattern of singling out religious minorities for persecution. The Holocaust, for example, witnessed the systematic targeting and extermination of six million Jews by the Nazis. The Armenian Genocide, too, saw the

Ottoman Empire specifically targeting the Armenian Christian population, resulting in the death of approximately 1.5 million people. Similarly, the Rwandan Genocide witnessed the targeting of Tutsis, who were predominantly Christian, by the Hutu majority.

Religious persecution during genocides is often fueled by a combination of factors, including religious intolerance, ethnic tensions, and political ideologies. In many cases, religious minorities are seen as a threat to the dominant group's identity, leading to their exclusion, marginalization, and ultimately, their extermination. This systematic targeting of religious minorities is a clear violation of human rights and highlights the interconnectedness of genocide and religious discrimination.

Understanding the experiences of religious minorities during genocides is essential in comprehending the full extent of the horrors they endured. Their stories, testimonies, and survival narratives provide invaluable insights into the complex dynamics of genocidal violence. Examining the specific targeting and experiences of different religious groups, such as Jews, Armenians, and Tutsis, allows historians and researchers to shed light on the various forms of persecution they faced, including forced conversions, mass killings, sexual violence, and forced displacement.

Furthermore, exploring the legal frameworks and mechanisms related to prosecuting genocidal crimes and seeking justice for victims is crucial in addressing the aftermath of religious persecution during genocides. The role of international law in holding perpetrators accountable, seeking reparations, and preventing future genocides is a topic of significant importance for historians and those interested in genocide prevention and intervention.

Religious persecution during genocides leaves a lasting impact on collective memory and commemoration. The role of memorials, museums, education, and media representation in ensuring that the stories of religious minorities are not forgotten is a critical aspect of understanding the long-term consequences of genocidal violence.

In conclusion, religious persecution targeting religious minorities during genocides is a significant and deeply troubling aspect of historical genocides. It is an important subchapter that addresses the experiences of religious minorities, the legal implications, and the long-term impact on collective memory and human rights. By examining these aspects, historians can contribute to a deeper understanding of the complexities of genocidal violence and work towards preventing future instances of religious persecution.

Right to Life and Security: Genocide as the Ultimate Violation of Human Rights

Genocide is undoubtedly one of the most horrifying atrocities committed throughout history. It represents the ultimate violation of human rights, specifically the right to life and security. This subchapter delves into the devastating impact of genocide on individuals and societies, examining the historical instances of genocide and their profound implications for humanity.

Drawing upon specific instances such as the Holocaust, Armenian Genocide, and Rwandan Genocide, this subchapter provides a comprehensive analysis of the targeted destruction of particular ethnic, religious, or racial groups. By exploring the historical context, causes, and consequences of these genocides, historians gain a deeper understanding of the complexities surrounding this grave violation of human rights.

Moreover, this subchapter sheds light on the phenomenon of genocide denial and revisionism. It examines the troubling tendency of some individuals or groups to deny or revise the historical occurrence of genocides. By delving into the motivations and implications of denial and revisionism, historians can better understand the challenges faced in acknowledging and addressing genocidal crimes.

Furthermore, this subchapter explores strategies and initiatives aimed at preventing and intervening in instances of genocide. By analyzing past and present efforts, historians gain valuable insights into the complexities of genocide prevention, including the role of international law and intervention.

The subchapter also emphasizes the importance of amplifying the voices of genocide survivors and sharing their stories. By highlighting the experiences and testimonies of survivors from different genocides, historians provide a platform for these individuals to bear witness and contribute to the collective memory of humanity.

Additionally, this subchapter delves into the legal frameworks and mechanisms related to prosecuting genocidal crimes and seeking justice for victims. It examines the challenges and progress made in holding perpetrators accountable, illustrating the vital role of international law in addressing the aftermath of genocide.

Finally, the subchapter explores the lasting impact of genocides on human rights, including issues of ethnic and religious discrimination. It discusses how these violations continue to shape societal structures and relationships, emphasizing the importance of promoting equality and combating discrimination in post-genocide societies.

In conclusion, this subchapter serves as a comprehensive exploration of the connection between genocide and human rights. By providing historical context, analyzing legal frameworks, and amplifying survivor voices, historians gain valuable insights into the profound impact of genocides on humanity. Through this understanding, they contribute to the prevention of future atrocities and the pursuit of justice for victims.

Chapter 7: Genocide and Collective Memory: Exploring How Societies Remember and Commemorate Genocides, Including the Role of Memorials, Museums, and Education

Commemoration and Memorialization: Ensuring the Memory of Genocide Victims

In the wake of horrific genocides throughout history, it is essential to ensure that the memory of the victims is commemorated and memorialized. By doing so, we not only honor the lives lost but also strive to prevent such atrocities from happening again. Commemoration and memorialization play a crucial role in the collective memory of societies, helping to educate future generations and promote a culture of remembrance.

Memorials and museums have become powerful tools for preserving the memory of genocide victims. These physical spaces serve as solemn reminders of the atrocities committed and provide a platform for survivors to share their stories. By visiting these memorials, historians can gain a deeper understanding of the complexities and consequences of genocides, which can inform their research and scholarship.

Education also plays a vital role in ensuring the memory of genocide victims. By including the study of genocides in school curricula, historians can contribute to the preservation of memory. Education fosters empathy and critical thinking, enabling students to recognize the warning signs and actively work towards preventing future genocides. It is through education that the lessons of history can be passed down to future generations, ensuring that the memory of genocide victims remains alive.

Additionally, the media, including films, documentaries, and literature can significantly impact how genocides are remembered. Historians can contribute to this aspect by analyzing and critiquing media representations of genocides. By highlighting accurate and responsible portrayals, historians can contribute to a more informed public discourse and challenge any attempts at revisionism or denial.

Furthermore, commemoration and memorialization can be deeply intertwined with efforts towards reconciliation and healing in post-genocide societies. Historians can explore truth and reconciliation commissions and other initiatives aimed at fostering dialogue and understanding between survivors, perpetrators, and their respective communities. By examining the complexities of reconciliation processes, historians can shed light on the challenges and successes in post-genocide societies.

In conclusion, commemoration and memorialization are essential in ensuring the memory of genocide victims. Historians play a critical role in this process by conducting research, analyzing media representations, and contributing to educational initiatives. By actively engaging with the subchapter on commemoration and memorialization, historians can contribute to the preservation of memory, promote understanding, and prevent the recurrence of genocides.

Museums and Exhibitions: Educating the Public about Genocidal Atrocities

Introduction:

Museums and exhibitions play a vital role in educating the public about genocidal atrocities, serving as powerful tools for understanding the historical context, impact, and consequences of these horrific events. By preserving and curating artifacts, testimonies, and narratives, museums provide invaluable spaces for remembrance, commemoration, and educational engagement. This subchapter delves into the significance and impact of museums and exhibitions in educating the public about genocidal atrocities, highlighting their role in promoting understanding, empathy, and preventing future acts of genocide.

1. The Power of Museums and Exhibitions:

Museums and exhibitions create immersive experiences that enable visitors to engage with the history and the human stories behind genocidal atrocities. By showcasing artifacts, photographs, and personal testimonies, they provide a tangible connection to the past, fostering empathy and understanding. Moreover, multimedia installations, interactive displays, and curated narratives help convey complex historical information in an accessible and engaging manner.

2. Museums as Educational Institutions:

Museums serve as educational institutions that go beyond traditional classroom settings. By collaborating with scholars, researchers, and survivors, they offer unique insights into the causes, processes, and repercussions of genocides. Exhibitions provide a space for critical examination and reflection, challenging visitors to confront difficult truths and question their own assumptions.

3. Preserving Collective Memory:

Museums and exhibitions contribute to the preservation of collective memory, ensuring that future generations remember the victims and understand the importance of preventing such atrocities from happening again. By documenting and archiving historical evidence, museums become custodians of truth, countering denial and revisionism.

4. Promoting Dialogue and Healing:

Museums and exhibitions also serve as platforms for dialogue and healing, bringing together survivors, descendants, and communities affected by genocidal atrocities. Through public programs, lectures, and workshops, they facilitate discussions on issues such as reconciliation, justice, and human rights, fostering understanding and empathy.

Conclusion:

Museums and exhibitions are indispensable in the educational process of understanding and preventing genocidal atrocities. By providing spaces for reflection, fostering empathy, and preserving collective memory, these institutions play a crucial role in ensuring that the lessons of history are learned, and that the horrors of the past are not repeated. As historians, we have a responsibility to support and promote these initiatives, as they contribute to both our understanding of the past and our commitment to a more just and peaceful future.

Education and Curriculum: Teaching Genocide History and Promoting Tolerance

In recent years, there has been a growing recognition of the importance of teaching genocide history as a means to promote tolerance and prevent future atrocities. This subchapter aims to explore the significance of including genocide education in the curriculum and its implications for fostering a more inclusive and compassionate society.

Historical genocides have left a profound impact on humanity, and it is crucial that historians delve into specific instances of genocide, such as the Holocaust, Armenian Genocide, or Rwandan Genocide. By studying these atrocities in detail, we can uncover the truth behind these events and understand their causes, consequences, and broader historical context. This knowledge is essential for historians specializing in historical genocides, equipping them with the tools to analyze and interpret these events accurately.

Moreover, this subchapter will also examine the phenomenon of genocide denial and revisionism. By exploring the motivations and tactics employed by individuals or groups attempting to revise or deny the historical occurrence of genocides, historians can expose the dangers of such revisionist ideologies and shed light on the importance of historical accuracy and integrity.

In the realm of education, this subchapter will discuss strategies and initiatives aimed at teaching genocide history and promoting tolerance. By integrating genocide education into the curriculum, educators can ensure that future generations are aware of the atrocities committed in the past and develop a sense of empathy and understanding towards different cultures and ethnicities. It will highlight the need for comprehensive and age-appropriate curricula that incorporate survivor testimonies, historical documents, and multimedia resources to engage students and facilitate their learning.

Additionally, this subchapter will explore the impact of genocide on human rights and discuss the legal frameworks and mechanisms related to prosecuting genocidal crimes and seeking justice for victims. It will also delve into the role of memorials, museums, and education in collective memory and how societies remember and commemorate genocides.

By addressing these topics, this subchapter aims to provide historians with valuable insights into the significance of teaching genocide history and promoting tolerance. Through education and an understanding of past atrocities, we can foster a more compassionate and inclusive society, one that is committed to preventing future acts of genocide and upholding human rights.

Chapter 8: Genocide and Gender: Investigating the Specific Targeting and Experiences of Different Genders during Genocides, Including Sexual Violence as a Weapon of Genocide

Gendercide: The Systematic Killing of a Specific Gender Group

In the dark annals of history, genocides have left an indelible mark on humanity. The Holocaust, Armenian Genocide, and Rwandan Genocide are among the most notorious instances that have haunted our collective consciousness. However, beyond the general discussion of genocides, it is essential to delve into the specific targeting and experiences of different genders during these atrocities.

Gendercide, the systematic killing of a specific gender group, has been an often overlooked aspect of genocides. While genocides have primarily targeted ethnic or religious groups, gender has played a significant role in the selection of victims, particularly women. Sexual violence has been employed as a devastating weapon of genocide, leaving long-lasting physical, emotional, and psychological scars on survivors.

This subchapter aims to shed light on the gender-specific dimensions of genocides throughout history. By examining the experiences of women and men, we can gain a deeper understanding of the complexities and horrors inflicted upon different gender groups. It is crucial to recognize that gendercide is not limited to one particular genocide but transcends time and geographical boundaries.

Through the analysis of primary sources, survivor testimonies, and scholarly research, this subchapter will explore the specific targeting, persecution, and experiences of different genders during genocides. By acknowledging the gendered aspects of these atrocities, historians can contribute to a more comprehensive understanding of the dynamics at play and the impact on both individuals and societies.

Moreover, this subchapter seeks to address the intersectionality of gender with other factors such as ethnicity, religion, and social status. The experiences of women and men during genocides are influenced by multiple identities, and understanding these complexities is crucial in unraveling the full extent of the crimes committed.

By examining gendercide within the broader context of historical genocides, this subchapter aims to contribute to the ongoing dialogue among historians and scholars. It also serves as a call to action, emphasizing the importance of recognizing and addressing the specific targeting of gender groups during genocides. Through increased awareness, education, and research, we can strive to prevent such atrocities from occurring in the future while honoring the memory of those who have suffered and perished.

In the pursuit of truth and justice, it is imperative that historians and scholars continue to uncover the hidden narratives of gendercide, amplifying the voices of survivors and shedding light on this dark chapter of human history. By doing so, we can ensure that the victims are not forgotten and that their stories serve as a powerful reminder of the urgent need to prevent and intervene in instances of genocide.

Sexual Violence as a Weapon: Rape and Sexual Abuse during Genocides

Sexual violence has been a devastating and prevalent aspect of genocides throughout history. In this subchapter, we will delve into the disturbing reality of rape and sexual abuse as weapons used during genocides, shedding light on the experiences of victims and the long-lasting impact on humanity.

Examining specific instances of genocide, such as the Holocaust, Armenian Genocide, or Rwandan Genocide, we will uncover the systematic use of sexual violence as a tool to humiliate, control, and destroy targeted populations. By exploring survivor testimonies and historical records, we will gain a deeper understanding of the extent and brutality of these acts.

Understanding the phenomenon of sexual violence as a weapon of genocide is crucial for historians and scholars in the field of historical genocides. By analyzing the specific targeting and experiences of different genders during genocides, we can unravel the complexities of these atrocities and their long-term effects on survivors and their communities.

Furthermore, we will discuss the role of sexual violence in perpetuating cycles of trauma, as well as the challenges faced by survivors in seeking justice and healing. By bringing attention to this aspect of genocides, we hope to contribute to ongoing discussions on genocide prevention and intervention, as well as the prosecution of genocidal crimes.

Additionally, we will examine the impact of sexual violence on human rights, including issues of ethnic and religious discrimination. By highlighting the unique struggles faced by survivors, we aim to foster a deeper understanding of the intersections between gender, genocide, and human rights.

Lastly, we will explore the role of sexual violence in post-genocide societies and the efforts towards reconciliation and healing. By understanding the specific experiences of survivors, we can better support their journey towards justice and contribute to the reconciliation process.

This subchapter aims to provide historians with a comprehensive understanding of the use of sexual violence as a weapon during genocides. By shedding light on this overlooked aspect of genocidal atrocities, we hope to foster critical discussions, challenge denial and revisionism, and contribute to the prevention of future genocides.

Gender Dynamics: Analyzing the Roles and Experiences of Men, Women, and LGBTQ+ Individuals

In the study of historical genocides, it is crucial to analyze the roles and experiences of different genders and sexual orientations. This subchapter aims to shed light on the specific targeting and experiences of men, women, and LGBTQ+ individuals during genocides, and how their stories have shaped our understanding of these tragic events.

Throughout history, genocides have often targeted specific groups based on their gender or sexual orientation. For example, during the Holocaust, LGBTQ+ individuals were subjected to persecution and extermination alongside other marginalized groups. Similarly, in the Rwandan Genocide, women were specifically targeted for sexual violence as a weapon of genocide. Understanding these dynamics is essential to comprehending the full extent of genocidal atrocities.

By examining the roles and experiences of men, women, and LGBTQ+ individuals during genocides, historians can gain insight into the power structures and social hierarchies that contribute to these mass killings. It provides an opportunity to challenge the traditional narratives that often overlook the unique experiences of marginalized groups. This subchapter encourages historians to delve deeper into these stories and amplify the voices of those who have been historically silenced.

Moreover, understanding the gender dynamics in genocides is crucial for promoting justice and reconciliation in post-genocide societies. By acknowledging the specific forms of violence and oppression faced by different genders, we can work towards a more inclusive and empathetic approach to healing and reconciliation. This subchapter also explores the efforts towards reconciliation and healing, including truth and reconciliation commissions, that have been implemented in various post-genocide societies.

Additionally, this subchapter highlights the importance of media representation in shaping our collective memory of genocides. It explores how genocides are represented in various forms of media, including films, documentaries, and literature. By critically analyzing these representations, historians can challenge stereotypes and misconceptions, and ensure a more accurate understanding of the gender dynamics within genocides.

In conclusion, this subchapter serves as a call to action for historians to analyze and understand the roles and experiences of men, women, and LGBTQ+ individuals during genocides. By doing so, we can contribute to a more comprehensive and nuanced understanding of historical genocides, and work towards preventing future atrocities through education, advocacy, and justice for victims.

Chapter 9: Genocide and Reconciliation: Examining Efforts towards Reconciliation and Healing in Post-Genocide Societies, Including Truth and Reconciliation Commissions

Truth and Reconciliation Commissions: Facilitating Healing and Justice after Genocides

In the aftermath of genocides, societies are left shattered and traumatized, struggling to come to terms with the horrors they have endured. The process of healing and seeking justice is a complex and delicate one, requiring careful navigation of the truth and reconciliation. This subchapter explores the role of Truth and Reconciliation Commissions (TRCs) in facilitating healing and justice after genocides.

TRCs have emerged as powerful mechanisms for post-genocide societies to confront their painful past and move forward towards a more just and reconciled future. These commissions provide a platform for victims and perpetrators to share their experiences and narratives, fostering a deeper understanding of the causes and consequences of the genocide. By acknowledging the truth, societies can begin to heal the wounds inflicted upon them.

One of the primary objectives of TRCs is to offer a space for victims to tell their stories and have their voices heard. Survivors of genocides often carry the burden of their traumatic experiences, and the opportunity to share their stories can be cathartic and empowering. Through public testimonies, victims reclaim their agency and challenge the culture of silence that often surrounds genocidal events.

Moreover, TRCs play a crucial role in shaping collective memory and ensuring that the atrocities committed during genocides are not forgotten. By documenting and archiving testimonies, TRCs provide valuable historical records that can serve as a foundation for education and remembrance. This helps prevent the recurrence of genocides and promotes a culture of tolerance and empathy.

In addition to truth-telling, TRCs also aim to promote justice and accountability. While they do not have the power to prosecute individuals for their crimes, they often recommend legal actions based on their findings. By exposing the truth and identifying those responsible, TRCs contribute to the pursuit of justice for the victims.

However, it is important to recognize the limitations of TRCs. They are not a panacea for all the complexities and challenges faced by post-genocide societies. Critics argue that TRCs may undermine the pursuit of criminal justice by offering amnesty to perpetrators who confess their crimes. Furthermore, the effectiveness of TRCs in achieving lasting reconciliation and healing is still a subject of debate.

Nonetheless, Truth and Reconciliation Commissions have proven to be valuable mechanisms in post-genocide societies. Their role in facilitating healing, justice, and collective memory cannot be underestimated. By addressing the painful past, these commissions contribute to the prevention of future genocides and the promotion of a more compassionate and just world.

Reparations and Compensation: Addressing the Material and Psychological Impact of Genocides

Introduction:

The aftermath of genocides extends far beyond the immediate loss of life and destruction. The material and psychological impacts on survivors and their descendants are profound and long-lasting. This subchapter explores the importance of reparations and compensation in addressing these impacts and providing justice to the victims of historical genocides.

Material Impact:

Genocides result in the displacement, dispossession, and destruction of entire communities. The loss of property, land, and livelihoods leaves survivors in a state of extreme vulnerability. Reparations, including financial compensation, restitution of land, and access to resources, can help rebuild shattered lives and communities. By addressing the material impact of genocides, reparations can contribute to the process of rebuilding and recovery.

Psychological Impact:

Beyond the material losses, genocides inflict deep psychological wounds on survivors. The trauma experienced during genocides may lead to long-term mental health issues such as post-traumatic stress disorder, depression, and anxiety. Reparations and compensation should also address the psychological impact of genocides, providing survivors with access to mental health services, counseling, and support networks. Healing the psychological wounds is crucial for survivors to rebuild their lives and reclaim their agency.

Challenges and Controversies:

Implementing reparations and compensation schemes for historical genocides is not without challenges and controversies. Some argue that it is impossible to fully compensate for the loss of lives and the destruction of entire communities. Others question the responsibility of current generations for the atrocities committed in the past. Additionally, determining who should be eligible for reparations and how to distribute them fairly can be complex. These challenges require careful consideration and engagement with all stakeholders involved.

Lessons from Past Efforts:

Despite the challenges, there have been successful examples of reparations and compensation initiatives in post-genocide societies. The experiences of Holocaust survivors in receiving reparations from Germany and the struggles and successes of the Rwandan government in providing reparations to survivors of the Rwandan Genocide offer valuable lessons. These examples demonstrate the importance of political will, international cooperation, and a comprehensive approach to addressing both material and psychological impacts.

Conclusion:

Reparations and compensation are essential components of addressing the material and psychological impact of genocides. By acknowledging the suffering of survivors, providing support for their recovery, and seeking justice, reparations contribute to the process of healing and reconciliation in post-genocide societies. While challenges and controversies exist, the lessons learned from past efforts can guide future initiatives toward a more just and inclusive world. It is imperative for historians and those interested in historical genocides to advocate for reparations and compensation as a means of acknowledging the atrocities of the past and working towards a better future.

Rebuilding Trust and Social Cohesion: Promoting Dialogue and Understanding among Divided Communities

In the aftermath of a genocide, societies are often left shattered and deeply divided. Rebuilding trust and social cohesion becomes an imperative task to prevent further violence and ensure a sustainable peace. This subchapter aims to explore the importance of promoting dialogue and understanding among divided communities as a means to heal the wounds of historical genocides and foster reconciliation.

The legacy of historical genocides, such as the Holocaust, Armenian Genocide, or Rwandan Genocide, continues to affect societies today. Deep-rooted mistrust, trauma, and the persistence of intergenerational pain hinder efforts towards reconciliation. However, through promoting dialogue and understanding, it is possible to bridge these divides and lay the foundation for a harmonious coexistence.

Dialogue plays a crucial role in the process of healing and rebuilding trust. By creating safe spaces for survivors, perpetrators, and their descendants to share their stories and experiences, it becomes possible to create empathy and understanding. Through open and honest conversations, communities can begin to acknowledge the pain and suffering of all parties involved, fostering empathy and compassion.

Understanding is another key element in rebuilding trust and social cohesion. By educating communities about the historical context, causes, and consequences of genocides, a deeper understanding of the complexities of these events can be achieved. Historians play a vital role in this process, as they provide the necessary knowledge and expertise to shed light on the truth.

Initiatives such as truth and reconciliation commissions have been successful in fostering dialogue and understanding in post-genocide societies. These commissions provide a platform for victims, perpetrators, and bystanders to come forward, share their experiences, and seek justice. Through this process, individuals are given the opportunity to confront their past actions, apologize, and seek forgiveness, leading to a path of reconciliation.

Furthermore, education, memorialization, and commemoration also play a significant role in promoting dialogue and understanding. By integrating the history of genocides into school curriculums and creating museums and memorials, societies can ensure that the truth is never forgotten. These initiatives create spaces for dialogue and remembrance, allowing for a collective understanding of the atrocities committed.

In conclusion, rebuilding trust and social cohesion among divided communities is a challenging but necessary task in the aftermath of historical genocides. By promoting dialogue and understanding, societies can begin to heal, reconcile, and ensure that the painful lessons of the past are never forgotten. Historians, with their expertise and knowledge, have a crucial role to play in this process, providing the necessary context and truth that can pave the way for a more peaceful and inclusive future.

Chapter 10: Genocide and Media Representation: Analyzing How Genocides Are Represented in Various Forms of Media, Including Films, Documentaries, and Literature

Film and Documentaries: Portraying Genocidal Atrocities and Their Impact on Humanity

Films and documentaries have played a crucial role in shedding light on historical genocides and their lasting impact on humanity. Through powerful storytelling and visual imagery, these mediums have the ability to capture the horrors of genocidal atrocities and convey the experiences of both the victims and the perpetrators. This subchapter will explore the significance of films and documentaries in portraying genocidal atrocities and their impact on humanity, as well as the ethical considerations and challenges faced by filmmakers in this sensitive field.

Films and documentaries provide a unique platform for historians to reach a wider audience and educate them about specific instances of genocide, such as the Holocaust, Armenian Genocide, or Rwandan Genocide. By presenting historical events in a visual and emotive manner, these mediums allow viewers to connect with the human stories behind the statistics and comprehend the magnitude of these atrocities. Through evocative imagery and personal testimonies, films and documentaries can evoke empathy, stimulate critical thinking, and encourage a deeper understanding of the complexities surrounding genocidal crimes.

However, filmmakers must navigate ethical considerations when portraying genocidal atrocities. They must strike a balance between accurately representing historical events and avoiding gratuitous violence or sensationalism. The responsibility lies in presenting the truth without exploiting the suffering of the victims. This requires extensive research, consultation with survivors and experts, and a commitment to maintaining historical accuracy.

Furthermore, films and documentaries have the potential to shape public opinion and contribute to genocide prevention and intervention efforts. By amplifying the voices of survivors and exposing the consequences of hatred and intolerance, these mediums can inspire action and mobilize support for initiatives aimed at preventing future genocides. They can also serve as a tool for advocacy and raising awareness about ongoing genocides or instances of genocide denial and revisionism.

In addition, films and documentaries play a crucial role in preserving the collective memory of genocides. They contribute to the commemoration of victims, the education of future generations, and the preservation of historical truth. By portraying the atrocities committed during genocides, these mediums challenge societal amnesia and foster a culture of remembrance and reflection.

Overall, films and documentaries have the power to bring genocidal atrocities to life, evoke empathy, and contribute to the understanding, prevention, and healing of genocidal crimes. As historians, it is essential to recognize the significance of these mediums in portraying the truths of the past and ensure their responsible and ethical use in shaping the collective memory of humanity.

Literature and Fiction: Imagining the Unimaginable - Genocide Narratives in Literature

Throughout history, literature has played a crucial role in shaping our understanding of genocides and their impact on humanity. This subchapter explores the power of literature and fiction in capturing the unimaginable horrors of genocides and providing a platform for survivors to share their stories.

Literature has the unique ability to transport readers to different times and places, allowing them to experience the atrocities of genocides firsthand. Through vivid descriptions, compelling characters, and emotional narratives, authors can evoke empathy and create a deeper understanding of the human suffering endured during these dark periods of history.

Within the realm of historical genocides, authors have delved into specific instances such as the Holocaust, Armenian Genocide, and Rwandan Genocide, shedding light on the lesser-known aspects and individual stories that might otherwise be overlooked. By bringing these narratives to the forefront, literature has played a crucial role in preserving the memory of these genocides and ensuring that they are never forgotten.

Moreover, literature has also been a powerful tool in challenging genocide denial and revisionism. By presenting well-researched and carefully crafted narratives, authors can counter false narratives and provide evidence of the historical occurrence of genocides. Fiction, in its ability to engage and captivate readers, can effectively dismantle revisionist narratives and expose the truth.

Literature has also been instrumental in exploring strategies for genocide prevention and intervention. By portraying the consequences of inaction and the importance of early intervention, authors can inspire readers to take a proactive stance against genocide. Through their narratives, they highlight the urgent need for international cooperation, peacekeeping efforts, and the protection of vulnerable populations.

Finally, literature serves as a platform for genocide survivors to share their stories and experiences. By giving voice to those who have endured unimaginable hardships, authors provide a space for healing, remembrance, and empowerment. These narratives not only honor the resilience of survivors but also serve as a call to action for justice and accountability.

In conclusion, the subchapter on "Literature and Fiction: Imagining the Unimaginable - Genocide Narratives in Literature" highlights the profound impact of literature in shaping our understanding of genocides. From historical accounts to challenging denial and revisionism, literature has the power to educate, inspire, and commemorate. By exploring the narratives crafted by authors, historians gain a deeper appreciation for the role of literature in unearthing the truth and ensuring that the horrors of genocide are never forgotten.

Media Responsibility: Ethical Considerations in Depicting Genocidal Events and Their Aftermath

Introduction:

In the era of mass media, the responsibility of accurately representing and depicting genocidal events and their aftermath is of paramount importance. This subchapter will delve into the ethical considerations that media professionals and content creators should bear in mind when tackling such sensitive subjects. By exploring the impact of media representation on historical genocides, this subchapter aims to shed light on the potential consequences and responsibilities of media practitioners towards the survivors, victims, and the wider audience.

Understanding the Power of Media:

Media, in its various forms, possesses immense power to shape public opinion and influence collective memory. The images, narratives, and emotions conveyed by the media have the ability to either accurately portray the horrors of genocide or perpetuate harmful stereotypes and misconceptions. Therefore, it is crucial for media professionals to approach the depiction of genocidal events and their aftermath with sensitivity, accuracy, and empathy.

Balancing Historical Accuracy and Sensationalism:

One of the key ethical considerations in media representation of genocides is striking a balance between historical accuracy and sensationalism. While it is essential to provide factual information and historical context, media should avoid exploiting the traumatic experiences of survivors or sensationalizing the violence for commercial gain. Responsible media practitioners must prioritize the dignity and well-being of survivors and victims, ensuring their stories are told with sensitivity and respect.

Avoiding Perpetuation of Harmful Stereotypes:

Media representation of genocidal events should be mindful of avoiding the perpetuation of harmful stereotypes and biases. By adhering to ethical guidelines, media can challenge and dismantle stereotypes that contribute to the dehumanization of certain groups. Accurate and unbiased portrayals can foster empathy, encourage critical thinking, and promote understanding among audiences.

Promoting Healing and Reconciliation:

Media has the potential to contribute to healing and reconciliation in post-genocide societies. By giving voice to survivors and highlighting their stories, media representation can facilitate acknowledgment, understanding, and empathy. Responsible media practitioners should also explore narratives of reconciliation and efforts towards healing, showcasing the resilience and determination of affected communities.

Conclusion:

The media holds a profound responsibility in its portrayal of genocidal events and their aftermath. By adhering to ethical considerations, media practitioners can contribute to truth-telling, understanding, and empathy. Through responsible media representation, the power of storytelling can be harnessed to ensure that the lessons of history are learned, and the voices of survivors and victims are heard, respected, and remembered.